ANCHOR BOOKS

POETS' PRIDE IN THE SOUTH WEST

Edited by

Heather Killingray

First published in Great Britain in 1997 by
ANCHOR BOOKS
1-2 Wainman Road, Woodston,
Peterborough, PE2 7BU
Telephone (01733) 230761

All Rights Reserved

Copyright Contributors 1997

HB ISBN 1 85930 588 1
SB ISBN 1 85930 583 0

FOREWORD

Anchor Books is a small press, established in 1992, with the aim of promoting readable poetry to as wide an audience as possible.

We hope to establish an outlet for writers of poetry who may have struggled to see their work in print.

The poems presented here have been selected from many entries. Editing proved to be a difficult task and as the Editor, the final selection was mine.

Poets' Pride In The South West is a compilation of poetry which has been assembled using the work of poets who reside in this area.

The poems vary in style and content, ranging from what they like about their home town/city to pleasant memories they have about a particular aspect of life whilst living in the area.

Each poem in this collection is unique and shows the reader how proud they are to live in the South West.

An inspirational collection for one and all to read time and time again.

I trust this selection will delight and please the authors and all those who enjoy reading poetry.

Heather Killingray
Editor

CONTENTS

The Corn Tomb	Marcus Barrett	1
The Harbour	Andy Brelsford	2
Dreaming Of November	Jo Trehane	3
Drake's Devonshire	Richard Flemington	4
Holiday Devon	Janet Allwright	5
Memories And Dreams	Judi E Alban	6
Winter Dawn On		
Dawlish Seafront	J M Service	7
Devon	Beryl Jackman	8
Devon	Sheila Chappell	9
Views Along The Way	Jean Takle	10
Boyhood Memory	Jeff Stoddart	11
Teignmouth		
The River Estuary	Carol Dunn	12
Winter Boats	E Owens	14
Buckland Abbey	Sue Jenner	15
Venus De Phillack	Para	16
Estuary Vision -		
Kingsbridge, Devon	Elizabeth Ann Cleveland	18
Somerset Dreaming	Angela Alderton	19
On Pilgrimage?	Hannah Julian	20
Seascapes	Ann Linney	21
The Tristan Stone	Alan Brinsley	22
Cornwall	Michael Kent	23
Par Excellence	Margaret Phillips	24
The Heart Of Cornwall	Janis Priestley	25
Sennen Cove	Juliet Fowler	26
Cornwall	G E Burgess	27
Early Morning	Milly Saunders	28
Sea View	Gerry Blaxall	29
Remains To See	K P Watch	30
The Cornish Sea	Margaret Adams	31
The Lighthouse	Lavinia Drinkwater	32
Untitled	Julie Tippett	33
The Lizard	Keith Onslow	34
A Cornish Village	A M Dalley	35

Across The Valley	Louise Russell	36
My Cornwall	Susan Starkey	37
Why	Olive Brown	38
Walking To Lamorna	Nicholas B Taylor	40
Cornish Gold	Darren Willcock	42
Precious Memories	Jane Rennie	43
This Fair Devon	Linda Kernot	44
Fisherman's Cove	Steven Eddy	46
Cornish Winter	Elizabeth O'Hara	47
Cornwall	Elaine Tamblyn	48
Cornwall (Why Did No-one Hear?)	J Middleton	49
The Right Decision	John David Sams	50
A Cornish Spring	Maureen Davis	51
Storm 89	Alan P Polley	52
Hold A Toast To Devon's Boast	Stuart Higginson	53
Port Isaac Harbour	Amanda Aldridge	54
Cornwall	Bernice Runnalls	55
My Cornwall	R H Waters	56
Devon	Irene Tapper	57
Cream Of The Earth	May Dabrowiecki	58
Devon Delights	Helen Phillips	59
Take A Trip To Plymouth	Linda Casey	60
Devon	Sue Goss	61
Holbeton Point	Jean Jarrett	62
The Pride Of Devon	Merilyn Gulley	63
Devon	Christine Westgate	64
Wembury Bay	Lydia McCubbin	65
Pride Of Devon	Annie Starkey	66
The Farmer	Douglas Dart	67
Dartmoor	Anne Hague	68
Dartmoor	Carmen Weston	69
Devon	Elizabeth Mitchell	70
The Commuters	Adrian Evans	71
The Devon Countryside	Betty Colton	72
A Devon Farm	Glennis Horne	73
Devonshire Dumpling	Peggy Moore	74

Quilt Me A County	Marian Lancaster	75
Looking Westwards	Patricia Evans	76
My Devon	Yvette Mullis	77
The Whole Devon Scene	Jeanette Gaffney	78
Cranmere Pool	Steve Newbury	79
Three Miles Of Tamar	Nick Spargo	80
Silent Watcher	James Spargo	81
Devon Delights	Pearl Mansell	82
Bath In Bloom	Edna Pine	83
A Field In Somerset	J C Aston	84
Somerset Spring	Vera Dyer	85
Somerset	J Wenmoth	86
Our Town, Weston-Super-Mare	Dympna Slattery	87
Winter In The Abbey	Val Flint-Johnson	88
Zumerzet . . . Oooarrrr!	Louise Brown	89
Pride Of Somerset	F L Brain	90
Untitled	Joan E Bartlett	91
Devon's Jewel	Margaret Vincetn	92

THE CORN TOMB

I stumbled on that ripe cropped ground,
Its goldenness,
Where warring tribesmen once did pound,
In fearlessness,
And saw that which I'd hoped I'd find,
Such subtleness;
Stained deep there in a perfect round,
In clarity.

A blanched mark there did confound,
My eagerness,
As careless centuries so bedrowned,
The sacredness,
Of this warrior's once solid mound.
Such timelessness;
I stepped around his shape without a sound,
In amity.

Marcus Barrett

THE HARBOUR

The lone cry of a seagull
    Wakes me from my dream
As I gaze out on the harbour
    Thinking how it must have been.

Boats with sails all folded
    Would have lined the sandy shore,
Waiting for the tide's return
    To put to sea once more.

And old men, with many a tale to tell
    Must have sat, their nets a-mending
And old wives with hot suppers ready
    Would have stood in dark descending.

As lamps were lit in town above
    And common man's work was done
In the harbour and on ocean wave
    The fisherman's was begun.

Andy Brelsford

DREAMING OF NOVEMBER

I went to the cliffs the other day
And stood a footfall from the edge,
I felt the challenge of eternity
On that granite ledge, above the sweep of Lantic Bay.
November tore cruelly at my hair,
And on my lips, I tasted the salt kiss of the sea.
I deeply filled my lungs and I could swear
That this was the very god's exhaled air.
Here was the Cornwall that tourists rarely see,
The land that sets my spirit flying free,
Past the wheeling fulmars on outstretched wings,
To ride the thermals with the noble peregrine
And watch the storm reflected in his gilded eye.
The horizon hid behind a cloak of grey,
A steely, almost tangible disguise,
That masked the tumbled, cowering, ancient rocks
And merged the untamed sea and troubled sky.
Below, the ghostly crescent moon of sand
Shrouded in a veil of drifting spray,
Grappled with a gang of rowdy waves,
And sent their spumy offerings far inland.
Tatters snagged on stubborn thorns that clung
Stoically to the seaward-leaning earth,
And burdened the gossamer in the stunted gorse,
And bowled across the fields of bitten turf.
My soul is forever wrecked upon these shores,
Flotsam glad to find a resting place.
For when I close my dreamer's eyes;
Gone are the picture-postcard skies,
To be replaced by the tidal race and the breakers' welcome roar.
Mine is the Cornwall that needs no name,
And means much more than sculpted rock and soil.
A love; a longing; a pride in belonging,
That dwells in my marrow and flows through my veins.

Jo Trehane

DRAKE'S DEVONSHIRE

Dartmoor -
Vast, dramatic country canvas
Producing visual delights,
Charming the eyes of tourists
With successive striking sights.

Or: Devonshire's splendid coastline
Graced with places of renown,
Where all is calm and peaceful,
Far from the fret of town.

Remembered: historic Plymouth city,
Famed for all time by Francis Drake;
His orders bold, and gritty -
'Finish our game of bowls,' he said,
'Here, on fair Plymouth Hoe.
Then, lads, and only *then* we'll go:
Chanting our victory song,
Dispatching arrogant Armadas
Back to Spain where they belong!'

An attitude true Devonians
Treasure to this very day, saying:
'Welcome, hopeful visitors,
To our native shire of Devon,
Where you may find from time to time
A fleeting glimpse of heaven.

Talking with friends when you are home
Its praises, please, extol,
'We saw a piece of England's soil,
It gave us quite a thrill
To feel the soul of Francis Drake
In Devonshire lingers . . . still!'

Richard Flemington

HOLIDAY DEVON

Something inside has just moved me to write,
About lovely Devon Oh boy what a sight,
Such wonderful beauty for all to see,
Stretching for miles aboundingly,
See lovely flowers in full bloom,
All houses and villages they festoon.
Hanging baskets overflowing everywhere.
The visitors just have to stand and stare,
Our beautiful villages they adore,
Coming back each year to see some more,
The grockles with their boxes galore
They are never-ending, Oh look some more!
As soon as we turn the summer clock.
It's to our beaches that they do flock,
For a few short months they do descend.
Until the summer is at an end,
Slowly on their weary way they wend
With all their treasures that they have found,
Weighting them down homeward bound.
A wonderful summer once again,
From now on in we will have some rain.

Janet Allwright

MEMORIES AND DREAMS

Devon Oh Devon I see you still
Feel still the wind across the moors,
And although I may never return
I still see the curlew a-soar.
In my memory I can see
The sea whipped into a frenzy of foam
With seagulls high up on the wing
Like me, they always will roam.
I remember the path on the clifftop
Where daffodils abounded in spring
With violets peeping so very shyly
Listening to church bells ring.
The country lanes I used to walk
With hedgerows wearing a lacy veil
Of frothy white flowers (I know not their name)
Half hiding a red box for mail.
My dream was always a country cottage
Far from the crowds snuggled in thatch;
But that alas I never attained
For the door to Devon behind me latched.
Place of cream teas and tourists,
Place of cottages amid fields of green;
Wherever my life's path will take me
Strange sights I may have seen -
Always will I remember Devon.

Judi E Alban

WINTER DAWN ON DAWLISH SEAFRONT

In the cold birth of dawn can be seen a blueprint,
tinged with pink and silver, of creation.
Mallards, moorhens, and black swans paddle the stream
in the half-light; night not quite done; day not yet begun;
the sun striving to break through the darkened silver-blue
of a cloud-strewn, primordial sky high above me:
whilst the sea's rage stretches before me, each blink
of my still sleep-filled eyes recording the untamed savagery
of near-frozen waves born out of some ineffable commandment
given in an age before time, and yet also today, and yesterday,
and tomorrow . . . Waves come and go for all eternity, it seems,
in those dawn-caught seconds, with new-birthed light freckling
the white-gold specks of gale-raged spume sweeping unchecked
over the terracotta sun-flecked sand. Gulls, wild as the waves
themselves, straddle the crests of crashing water,
all gold and silver-edged, silhouetted proud as storm clouds
in the almost adult day. And red sandstone cliffs wait
with quiet understatement for the sea to claim them
in some other dawn, at some other time than ours . . .

This is the Devon unseen by the tourist, with his chips,
his caravan, and his 'kiss-me-quick' hat, who suns himself
on those red-gold beaches - thriving, not so much on beauty,
as on the slower pace of life, the indolent warmth,
and the friendliness of Devonians. In the summer, Devon
does her duty; but in winter she becomes herself again -
wild and free - moors and sea open themselves to the elements.
In winter, Devon is left alone to breathe once more;
to loose and lose the trappings of mankind, and to just *be*.

J M Service

DEVON

In a little part of Devon
      Not very far from home
Is the nearest place to heaven you will find.
      It's placed between the woods and hills
In a valley full of colour,
      And all the people living there are of the happiest kind
Thatched cottages are painted white.
      A brook runs through the street
And everyone seems so content
      No matter who you meet.
So come on down to Devon
      To relax and to unwind
In a valley full of colour . . .
      It's the nearest place to heaven you will find.

Beryl Jackman

DEVON

You have never ever seen
A countryside so fresh and green,
With hamlets dotted here and there
And people never seem to care
About the rush and tear of life,
But take it easy with no strife.

There's wooded slopes, meandering streams
And places only found in dreams.
Cathedrals built of mellow stone
With historic stories of their own.
The little cafes aim to please
And serve you wonderful cream teas.

Ponies wander with the sheep
On moors with places wild and steep.
Children play on sun-kissed sand
And lovers wander hand in hand.
There is no better place to be
Than Devon in the West Country.

Sheila Chappell

VIEWS ALONG THE WAY

'Would you like to come with me today; see the views along the way?
Exeter to Launceston along the new dual-carriageway.'

With gentle bends and easy climbs, the views spill either side
Like technicolour ribbons of a two-track travel-guide.
The banks are iced with primroses, topped with candled conifers -
Palest green and delicate . . . too beautiful for words.
Farms nestle in the valleys, tiny hamlets climb the slopes
Bearing churches on their shoulders - the hub of prayer and hopes.
The road does not seek attention - inviting me to look at the moor
And every curve in the highway brings a view I've not seen before.
There are none of the worries of town roads; no crossings, blind
                                              corners or lights,
Very few motorway bridges or roundabouts 'shouting' their rights.
It's April; there's sunshine and shower, on a road that seems built
                                              just for us -
Not a hint of a holiday queue, nor a glimpse of a sightseeing bus.
A Tornado crosses our vision and circles the roof of the moor,
Swept wings gracefully turning, our engine hum muting its roar.
A sparse wood we pass and my heart stills for, by trees that are
                                              mossy and gnarled,
I sense spirits that stand there in wonder, to gaze as we pass
                                              in our world.
And - over the border to Launceston; ruined castle on top of the hill -
Where the town tumbles down to the river in an ancient
                                              urban-type spill.

I should like you to come on the journey; see the views along the way -
Give praise to *the one* who deserves it - for enhancing the
                                              dual-carriageway.

Jean Takle

BOYHOOD MEMORY

The white blanket of winter had gone, giving way to spring
My child's eyes filled with wonder, and my heart began to sing
As I walked the lanes of my boyhood, full of gentleness and fun
My innocence like a beacon, shining brightly in the sun.

The pleasures that I knew cost little then, unlike today
Everything we do, dictated by the hand stretched out for pay.
Walking in the valleys of my youth, soft rain upon my face
Listening to the far church bells, a new-born lamb, a soft embrace.

Tadpoles in the twinkling brook, reading by the fire
Helping with a suckling calf, midnight in the old stone byre.
Days of magic, peace, and love, full of hope and joy,
Memories of yesterday, requiem for a golden boy.

The boy was stolen long ago, replaced now by the man.
Fading memories remain since that magic time began
Yet when spring returns, as she will, the joy is lived again
And troubles melt, like winter snow, sweet tears dull the pain.

My heart beats loud and sings again, when spring it has begun,
And the lost joy, of that long dead boy, stays burning . . . in the sun!

Jeff Stoddart

TEIGNMOUTH
THE RIVER ESTUARY

Towards the sea the river runs
Along the steep red cliffs
Where small boats moored move with the tides
And the aromatic mud does shift.

Fishes swans and all wildfowl
Do nestle in the banks
To share the ups and downs of water
For which they all give thanks.

The cormorant stands black and proud
As he waits for unsuspecting prey
The heron gull flies past with screech
To make for a noisy day.

A small pull-me boat is chained across
To get folk from side to side
To smell the salt and fresh sea air
And watch the moving tide.

Alongside it all there is the town
With its festivals, fun and dance
And resting places to quench your thirst
Making a visit here enhanced.

The old stone-faced cottages washed with salt
With the baskets of flowers they display
The effort a town in bloom goes through
To brighten up the day.

Then down to the beach to admire
The pebbles and the sand
To walk along the pier and prom
And listen to Sunday's band.

Then back to watch the tidal flow
Of the wonderful estuary
That empties out a river's thirst
Into the powerful sea.

Carol Dunn

WINTER BOATS

Topsham quay's a depressing sight,
The boats are in a wintry plight,
Up on dry land, away from the sea,
No-one for months now will they carry,

The tall masts pointing straight to the sky,
They sway and shimmer, and look very high,
Clinking and rattling in the evening breeze,
Longing to be sailing out over the seas,

Held up by blocks and timber as well,
Not sat in the water, taking the swell,
Sat still on dry land, not on the high seas,
It's a crime for yachts such as these,

But come the spring once more they'll be found,
Out on the water for foreign ports bound,
The sail billowing proudly, like a wing in the sky,
What a glorious sight, for one such as I.

E Owens

BUCKLAND ABBEY

Remotely set on the western fringe of Devon
Lies Buckland Abbey, a chequered history to its name.
Its most notorious owners were part of England's past -
Seadogs Grenville and Drake, of Elizabethan fame.

It started as an Abbey, founded by Amicia,
In loving memory of her spouse, the Earl of Devon.
The white monks worshipped there in tranquillity and peace.
That could bring them one step closer to their heaven.

The monastery fell in fifteen thirty-nine.
Grenville of Bideford was given the right to buy.
His son, Sir Roger, died aboard the 'Mary Rose'.
Young Richard favoured London, so let the Abbey lie.

He presented to Queen Bess a scheme to make her rich
But she refused to give permission for such a plan.
In frustration, he rode down to Buckland Abbey
And rebuilt it to befit a country gentleman.

He pulled down domestic buildings and the cloisters.
From the church an impressive Great Hall he did make.
He stayed there for a while and then returned to Stowe.
Buckland Grenville was mortgaged on to Francis Drake.

Plymothians they loved him and made him their Lord Mayor.
He brought water to the town through an open leat.
Soon, Queen and Country called him to sail to San Juan.
Drake met his end through sickness - his story was complete.

Buckland Abbey stands - Grenvilles and Drakes there no more,
It's for the artefacts that visitors do come.
But hark! For 'tis said, Drake will come back from the dead,
If he hears the beating of his battle-weary drum.

Sue Jenner

VENUS DE PHILLACK

As I roved out to Phillack strand
One dreamland in July
I met a girl in nature's dress
Upon a horse so high.

I followed over miles of sand,
All where the tide was low;
I followed where the stars were wet
And hoof prints bade me go.

The moon was in the mirror sand
And in the white-horsed sea,
When, all at once, the pale horse turned
And showed the girl to me.

I saw the fair hair in the wind,
The grey-green eyes alight;
I felt the moonbeam on her thigh
And found her breasts of white.

I asked my dream girl who she was
And why she rode so high.
She said: 'I come from far away
To find you by and by.

You have me now and for awhile
On beds of red and dew,
Yet we shall part for twenty years
And still be one, we two.

I'll meet you by a young child's grave
And tell you of my tears,
Before a life with laughter comes
To light our later years.

My love is strong as tide of moon on high;
There is no god but sunrise and the sea.
If you should leave the shore where once we were,
Return on foaming sand and love with me.'

Para

ESTUARY VISION - KINGSBRIDGE, DEVON

Estuary magic, springtime morning
Breeze transporting misty air
Sunshine through reflecting rigging
Waterglass is mirrored there
Dog and I just stand and stare.

Dippers probing on the shoreline
Mallards winking, faking sleep
Seagull voices pierce the hush,
Searching, floating, wheeling shriek.
Grebes are playing hide and seek.

Not a ripple on the surface
To disturb the early calm.
Stone-clad wharfs, iron mooring rings
Redshank screaming in alarm.
Wagtail struts with dipping wings
Looking for discarded things.

Eagrets scavenge murky pools
Ducks and moorhens have no rules.
Heron, still, with watchful eye
Searches flotsam drifting by.

Elizabeth Ann Cleveland

SOMERSET DREAMING

I can sit and see,
look skyward to be
Sure in my dreaming
I can paint life free

A dream is a plan
Without anchor stone
It flexes and bends
And moulds as your own

I can take it and shape it
Recall it and trawl it
I can wind it or bind it
Swirl it or twirl it

Let abundance soar
In creating galore
A castle of dreams
A bundle of schemes
If I choose to so roam
With a dream of my own

I can dream what I know
I can play as I go
I can take what I see
Without worry for me

For freedom is here
Within my mind's eye
Any web I can spiral
Any dream I can fly

> For a dream is elusive
> Not yet conclusive
> Still free to yield
> Still free to build

Angela Alderton

ON PILGRIMAGE?

Winding up through rain-dark fields
Passing old chapels of certainty by,
I turned to where rough cattle stood
Rumped up against a hedge
And shared an old communion,
Man with beast in the mire,
Heads sunk, weathering together.
Up then to the stony spine
Of an ancient hermetic track
Where human life thinned, I caught
Beneath the reek of soot-damped fires
The sudden stench of wild-blood spilt
Then heard a vixen's curdling cry.

My torch flickered, then went out.
I stood some time irresolute,
Night-blind and chilled with doubt,
Yearning not for a miracle
But for the shadow of a sign.
Then, adjusting to the dark
I discerned towards the East
More an emanation than a light,
Or mirage of my inner eye.
I should have known that the way
Of the spirit is never Romantic
- That self-deluding snare -
But a faint track easily lost,
For who knows where, or how, it lies.

Hannah Julian

SEASCAPES

I walked along the beach today,
I heard the seagulls cry,
The sand was warm beneath my feet,
The gentle breeze was but a sigh.

Small children played upon the sand,
They laughed and shouted out with glee,
Building sandcastles with their spades,
Running and splashing in the sea.

Small pebbles glinted on the shore,
The sun was warm upon my face
And granite cliffs beside me towered,
It was a very perfect place.

Today I walked along the beach,
The sky was grey above my head,
Great storm clouds gathered in the wind,
The sand was cold beneath my tread.

The wind whipped up the steel-grey sea,
Atlantic rollers, white-topped, rose
And crashed upon the pebbled shore,
Leaving their froth between my toes.

No children's happy voices heard,
No gulls with plaintive cry were there.
The beach deserted but for me
Walking with sea-spray in my hair.

O Cornwall, land of changing moods;
Of golden sand and blue-grey sea,
Of gulls and cliffs, sun, mist and storm,
This is the place I have to be.

Ann Linney

THE TRISTAN STONE

I passed you as I walked to Fowey,
Two hundred yards, at least.
You, silent, called;
I turned,
Wondering, half-ashamed,
Yet impelled:
Slowly back on the
Wayside turf
Till, close beside you,
Not knowing what to do,
But yet impelled,
I reached
(it was not far)
And pressed my palms
Against your rough, warm
Stone.
To give, or receive,
What?
In compassion, for Tristan,
And for Iseult?
To share in that caress
Some relic of your
Ill-starred love?
To soothe and be soothed?
Sentimental fool!
Yet I am glad
I turned back:
Your warm granite,
So hard, so soft,
Still tingles in my palms.
At least I tried
To bridge the gap.

Alan Brinsley

CORNWALL

So peaceful here in Cornwall
No noisy people
Everybody is friendly
Even to find the time to stop
And talk.

The hospital, where the staff
Are friendly to me, lies close to
The town.

Good shopping area, with
Many places to go
For entertainment.

Places (like Blantyre)
For people like me
To go to. Also
Colleges for learning.

The countryside is beautiful
With birds and animals,
Flowers everywhere.

There are many kinds of beaches
Some with lots of pebbles,
Surfing beaches, where surfers
Ride the waves.
I like to walk on the beaches
On warm sunny days,
Collecting stones, and shells,
Also visiting the gift shops
In caravan parks,
Where people come on holiday
And walk around the many footpaths, where you
Can see children swimming
With parents in the sea.

Michael Kent

PAR EXCELLENCE

Sitting with my back against the warm cliff,
I soon forget there had ever been a tiff.
Leaning back I feel the sun on my face
Of sea spray there's more than just a trace.
Golden grains of sand trickle through my fingers
An aroma of seaweed on nearby rocks faintly lingers,
The most peaceful sound is waves on the shore,
Not even disturbed by seagulls galore.
Daydreaming, dozing - more asleep than awake
Appreciating the chance to have this break,
My reverie has given me time to think;
But to the west the sun now sinks
So with reluctance I rise to leave -
Homeward bound my way to weave.
I stretch and gaze out over the bay
And then I spot the dolphins at play.
A wondrous sight - I'm under their spell -
Not only me - everyone else as well!
As they leap and dive, droplets glisten and gleam
Mesmerised, fascinated I stand in a dream.
They're not a rare sight along this coast,
But their effect on one is like seeing a ghost.
Surprise, disbelief, excitement and awe
Almost as if one's never really lived before.
With a flash of their tails they finish their game
Disappear out to sea as swift as they came.
Inspirational - beautiful - forever magical
Describes my home - just one word - *Cornwall!*

Margaret Phillips

THE HEART OF CORNWALL

From this window
the dark swell of Bodmin Moor
sprawls across the skyline -
intriguing, bewitching, enticing.

Occasionally,
between the close set trees,
a lance of searing sunlight
dissipates the density of that darkness.

Intrigued,
I observe, as a myriad dreams
(mythical emblems of unreality),
pass through its x-ray beams.

Bewitched,
I see the real and the imaginary,
intertwine, and hand in hand,
create allusive imagery.

Enticed,
I run towards that enchanted place,
longing to touch those shadows,
but like echoes they have left no trace.

A remote and ruthless moor
in a mystic but beautiful land.
Its darkness a strange metaphor
for all we do not understand.

Janis Priestley

SENNEN COVE

In its simplicity, in a dream
Of smuggling complicity
This cove reveals powerful rocks
Islanded by tortured waves;
While sands shine on its beach
Innocent, with their own curve
To an arc, sending an invitation
From their yellow wasted landscape
To smugglers, pirates, tourists.
Who can make a house
Lying between the tides
Safe with the fluxing
Sands forever or thinking
Itself safe, yet the grains run
Like a cascading waterfall . . .
And where would they land,
Not safely for themselves?
There are myriads of images
As Saint Sennen's cove is circled
With rocky hills of granite
Stark as in a reverberating enclosure.

Mist bedevils the Atlantic ocean
Shallowing into a white haze
On the tops of dark, unguarded
Currents, with the distant shadow
Of stretched roundness of bay
And cliff like an outlying trace
Of Sennen's secret and mysterious past.

Juliet Fowler

CORNWALL

Land of the grey stone and white river valley.
Land of the clay tips that heighten the view.
Wesleyan churches in primitive villages.
Ghosts of the past life still lingering there.

Quaint little villages with thatched roofed cottages.
Dew-laden meadow with cantering mare.
Cornish cream teas with a view 'cross the valley.
Meridian splendour in timeless luxure.

Flowers by the wayside in prolific splendour.
Primrose in the valley where the peace is serene.
Glimpse the pink campion 'midst the grass by the hedgerow.
Thrift on the cliff-tops where the view is sublime.

Newquay for surfing on Atlantic coast rollers.
Tintagel for legend, King Arthur of old.
Porthpean for sailing, (the spinnakers billowing).
Lanhydrock for fragrance the bluebells in spring.

Buzzards a-soaring, the cormorant skimmering.
The skylark ascending and singing on high,
The hawk powerfully hovering and dropping dramatically.
The swan gently sailing in harbour's reside.

Thoughts in conclusion

Where else can I go to find peace in the valley.
Where else can I go to find joy in my heart.
Where else can I go to seek the will of my Father.
Where can I go to be still with my Lord.

G E Burgess

EARLY MORNING
(Tresillian, Truro)

Morning light is slowly breaking,
Life is gently awakening,
Beautiful rays of light
Are spreading across the eastern sky;
Below the hills mighty sun still hides.
The clock is striking five.

Fresh morning spirit is prevailing,
Birds' chorus overwhelming,
Cattle grazing in surrounding meadows,
Badgers are returning to their environs.
Vixen is in a hurry,
To her cubs she must scurry.

From waste bins and cultivated land,
She provides cubs with many finds,
Moving with caution, care and heed,
Before the morning abates with speed.
Hedgehog searching on his track,
Playing and waiting at cat flap.

He desires something nice to feast,
Dogs and cats' leftovers at least.
Also many squirrels now appear,
Displaying aggressive attitudes;
They disperse poor finches and their brood,
Tits and robin must take refuge

Safety in old birch tree is at hand,
But they make a quick return to the feeding ground.
Now there is another sound,
Milkman is on his round,
Dog awakes perplexed,
As the clock strikes six.

Milly Saunders

SEA VIEW

A gilded image lying in the cleavage
Of rising hills,
Sunlight dancing to the rhythm of waves,
Tantalisingly out of reach
Not a sound can be heard, from the
Glittering silver sea,
Implanted as a jewel amidst the green.
Only a fleeting glimpse of this
Tinselled gem,
As I speed along the grey metal road.

Gerry Blaxall

REMAINS TO SEE

Look you over the dune land,
From cross, to cross beyond.
Know that in the between ground,
An ancient oratory lies buried,
For many years unseen.
A Celtic cross, old and grey,
Stands guard on what remains.
Of the Norman parish church,
Left now to ruin and decay.
The modern cross is sighted,
On somewhat higher ground.
To guide the earnest pilgrim,
Across the hallowed ground,
Within St Piran's bound.

K P Watch

THE CORNISH SEA

The moody sea
The melancholy sea
It beckons to me.
The petulant waves are choppy and cross
Black under the heavy sky
Its face is set to repel
But it beckons to me.

The smooth glassy sea
Calm and lazy
Idles onto the shore
Come swim if you wish
And be lulled by the lazy ripples,
Beckoning at the edge.

The tossing turbulent sea
Waves crashing and roaring
Bubbling white foam skimming the surface
Bouncing the surfers onto the shore
It calls to me.

The sea is a force to admire and respect
Stronger than you and me
The Cornish sea which has shaped our destiny.

Margaret Adams

The Lighthouse

The lighthouse at Godrevy
Guardian of St Ives bay.
Proud and erect upon the rocks
Its beacon showing the way.
Standing, it seems, in solitude
Out there in the sea
Like a sentinel on duty
Watching - endlessly.
Many a weary sailor
Follows its guiding light
Often a roving sea bird
Seeks refuge from long flight
Looking across Hayles' golden sands
Across to Carbis bay
Watching the seals and dolphins
Who often come to play.
In all kinds of weather
Working through the night
Silent in its mission
But the light forever bright.

Lavinia Drinkwater

UNTITLED

I admit defeat and lay down my pen,
unable to capture what Cornwall means to me
I sit back and watch the sea,

A silence echoes from the sky to the ground.
Unable to be defined. It dances all around
singing of heroes in ages long past,
lands full of magic - tales that still last
in the hearts and minds of men that can hear,
and feel, the memories living so near
to the lives they call now. This is Cornwall
with a rich magic for one and all
who long to discover it.

Julie Tippett

THE LIZARD

At the southern end of this great land, Landewednack the Lizard
stands, the sea surrounds its coast each side winds that blow and
never die, people there are hard and strong fishermen farmers tight
knit bond.

When nights are black and storms blow strong the ships at sea no
longer calm, people watch with bated breath and seek the flare that
lights the west, then the men with all their might run like mad
through the night to reach the craft so small and bold that fights the
waves, to save poor souls.

On returning to their homes, soaking wet with tired bones, loved
ones greet them all forlorn then cuddle each to keep them warm, in
the morning when the storm is spent you look for the men who to the
rescue went, not one you'll find to tell the tale, but those they saved,
remember well.

In this village at the end of the land, there's always someone to lend
a hand, no words are spoke of deeds they do they know somehow
their needs are few, when help is needed they have no fear, the
friends they have they hold very dear.

They have their church, the reading room their football club and
pub, paths to walk and songs to sing the Cornish rugby club, there's
always something here to do but strangers see it not, if only they sat
quietly they would see there's quite a lot.

So come and visit anytime enjoy our coastal paths, sit upon the
benches there and think of things long past, for those who come to
live with us please remember this, don't try to change the way we
are, we like it as it is.

Keith Onslow

A CORNISH VILLAGE

My name is Chapel Amble
An unassuming name.
It's lovely just to ramble
All through my leafy lanes.
I'm full of pretty houses
Unchanged throughout the years.
You'll never ever rouse me
From my quaint and sleepy ways
So many people love me
From far and wide they come.
To spend their precious holidays
And soak up our Cornish sun.
I hope they never change me
That progress never comes.
To wake me from my slumber
Should be never ever done.

A M Dalley

ACROSS THE VALLEY
(Memories of a Welsh Music Festival)

Warm July sunset,
Rich red-ochre glow
Way across the valley.
Smell of hay and beer and cigarettes
Wafting over the field.
The sound of shrieks of laughter,
A singer dancing on his chair.
Steady thud-thud-thud of drumbeats,
Someone's wailing the saddest song:
'Gabrielle twenty-five, where are you now?'
Voices everywhere, rising,
Mixing with the pollen in the floodlights;
Dusk is banished beyond our reach.
No night falls on the hilltop.
Can't hear a sound,
Only the noise.
Security men pacing the boundary
Don't know what they're missing.
All so young in that field,
Futures still unknowable.
Whether we stay or whether we go,
We'll always have this, our music.

Laughter in the artificial day -
Everyone is here, all the world:
We belong together.
And the steady thud-thud-thud of drumbeats,
They can hear us
Across the valley.

Louise Russell

MY CORNWALL

The granite of Cornwall is grey and bright,
The sea is clear blue and bright,
The fresh spring beech is green and bright,
The sunset is shining orange and bright.

Soft sand and big sandcastles,
Laughing children playing king of the castle,
Old and beautiful and eerie castles,
Hills and craggy cliffs topped with castles.

The primrose, bluebells and an early rose,
Lush green grass and every rose,
Lupins, fuchsias, flowers galore and the rose,
Brown, orange and reds colour the foliage and the rose.

Green hills and valleys serene and quiet,
Sheep grazing with their lambs, peaceful and quiet,
Cows walking into milking, slowly and quiet,
Tractors ploughing lonely and quiet.

Busy roads, chock-a-block with cars,
Village and towns full of cars,
Country lanes and speeding cars,
Car parks and theme parks full of cars.

Sea and shore battered with winds,
Trees and hedges blown by winds,
Black clouds, grey sky and winds,
Cold and bitter, those strong winds.

Back to summer, it soon comes in Cornwall,
Back in the fields, we're busy in Cornwall,
Back comes the cars, they bring money into Cornwall,
There's always something to do in my Cornwall.

Susan Starkey

WHY

Why do I live in Birmingham
I really cannot say
When all I want is a sunny beach
Beside a deep blue sea.

When my desires are the rugged cliffs
Of the lovely Cornish scene
Sea pinks, and Atlantic waves
Deep caves in which to dream

Of smugglers' deeds in days gone by
Of pirate ships and gold
King Arthur, Merlin, Guinevere
Until my blood runs cold.

Of Cornish pasties and cream teas
Of Starry Gazey pie
Of sharks swimming in the seas
And dolphins flying by.

Of cormorants and guillemots
And puffins nesting near
Of baby seals, and seagulls
And of Newquay's own steam beer.

Of Cornish mead and strawberry wine
And surfing in the sea
Of fishermen and lobster pots
And fresh caught crab for tea.

Of China clay and tin mines
And sea mists o'er the quay
Of lighthouses and hewer's huts
Gold sunsets out to sea.

If I could have one wish 'twould be
To live on Cornwall's shores
With the people I love best of all
In the place that I adore.

Olive Brown

Walking To Lamorna

Great rocks lay scattered like God's talcum powder
Round the cliff path as we walked to Lamorna.
Over the waves the foghorn sounded louder,
Gonging the noon as we rounded the corner.
Soft rain came easy as cream teas were calling,
Leaving the trail as the wind shook the hedges,
Crossing the wet fields with cow-pat feet squelching;
Finding our way by the towers of the churches.

Hard are these islands that lie on the backbone,
Standing out rough from the flesh of the west land;
Diving untamed through the crust of the ocean,
Ribs rising sheer from a beading of red sand.
Hard was the way as we walked to Lamorna.
Hard was the life of the men of the seashore.
Wealthy today with their flora and fauna,
They reach deep down still to the roots of before.

Dark towns remembered, their sure walls and columns
Cast shadows long as we walked to Lamorna.
In their wet alleys, ghosts dark-dressed and solemn
Joined silent voice in the praise of reformers.
In pits and caverns they founded their churches,
Worshipping strange gods of tin, wine and white clay,
Slipping with pure souls past devilish searches,
Through teeming night to the amnesty of day.

Back on the route in the clear of an evening,
Making our way through gorse, bramble and thicket;
Freed of its mist net the sun bird was gliding,
Pecking the shadows etching the pink granite.
Soon by a wide bay actors would be playing,
Striding the rocks in a timeless location,
High on the sea with a cold night breeze stirring;
Lights drifting slow through the full moon's reflection.

Soft rain blew in as we walked to Lamorna,
Misting the view of the mountain of angels.
Boats hauled up steep as we rounded the corner,
God's sand piles looming high over the gables.
Deep in the valley a river was running,
Playing a mill wheel with slow variation.
Think of the music when we'll be returning;
Ask only for the theme's reaffirmation.

Nicholas B Taylor

CORNISH GOLD

Clear white teeth
On a
Rural landscape,
Nationwide they mark our land.
Without their bite what would she be,
Akin to a normal English county?
Lost; a
Land without her gold.

Darren Willcock

PRECIOUS MEMORIES

Remembering Devon, when I was a lad.
An 'ansome county, it was by gad.
The 'oss and cart, rumbled along.
Us wid be singin', they ol' songs.
Pitchin' hay from dawn till dusk,
We was always in a rush.
To get they sheaves in, 'afore the rain
The weather always 'twas a pain.
Apple orchards full of fruit.
Pints of cider filled our boots.
Proper pasties, crimped round the edge.
Ate our dinner, 'neath that old hedge.
The village 'ad its local pub.
Post office and shop, they never shut.
Today 'tis modern, not like it was.
I really feels 'tis such a loss.
Most of my homeland, has now gone.
No one singin', they ol' songs.
Roads and bridges, whole new towns.
Really makes me want to frown.
I'll mind Devon, how it used to be.
When us admired, the beauty of a tree.
We worked 'ard, but enjoyed the day.
I really 'ave, nothin' more to say.

Jane Rennie

THIS FAIR DEVON

Of all the places I have been,
The towns and cities I have seen,
There's none that stirs such love and pride
As Devon's glorious countryside.

Wide open moors, a leaf-strewn lane,
The gentle touch of misty rain
That lays upon its dear-loved face
A fragile veil of fine-spun lace.

Wild rivers, ever rushing, flow
Through valleys where the bluebells grow;
Where ivy trails and willows weep
And snowdrops till the winter sleep.

Fine autumn rain, crisp winter sun,
In leafy woods where squirrels run.
A sleepy village, peaceful lies
'Neath lazy, drifting, summer skies.

Fresh morning dew, like silver pearls
Caresses fern that shyly curls;
A mossy carpet, newly spread,
And filtered sunlight overhead.

The church bells chime their blessèd call,
Come all ye faithful, one and all;
Come mother, daughter, father, son,
And praise the Lord for what He's done.

Steep, rocky cliffs and white-topped waves,
Strange tales of smugglers in secret caves;
And seagulls with their mournful cry
Trace circles through the winter sky.

Boat engines in the distance sound,
The fishermen are homeward bound;
The lighthouse flashes, all is well,
And through the stillness tolls a bell.

Dear Lord, if ever I should yearn
On foreign shores and hills to roam,
Let me, before I die, return
To this fair Devon, which is home.

Linda Kernot

FISHERMAN'S COVE

Sweet cove,
Golden sand, crystal water
Silvery fair maids and frisky seals.
Great, fern-shrouded cliff
A secret path across its chest.
An old fisherman's hut,
Ghostly picture of sturdy scaths
Strung across the bay,
Their restraining stacks stand idle.
Floating kestrels
And a skylark song,
Busy gulls hurry, meal to meal
High above lulling waters ebb and flow.
Free-minded bodies sit and chat,
Mainly locals, aware of its existence.
In the distance, fog-shrouded north cliffs loom,
An occasional yacht drifts by.
Within rock pools and inlets, seaweed gently rocks,
The great fronds shade a multitude of denizens
Busy with idle life.

Steven Eddy

CORNISH WINTER

Trees, their branches bleak and bare,
As the blasts of Cornish winter disturb the air.
Gales whip at rough-hewn cliffs outside the bay,
Relentlessly drenched by the salty sea spray.
Little boats nestle safely by the harbour's side,
Knowing that they're sheltered from the ravages of the tide.
The enigmatic sea looks dark and enraged.
In a battle with the lad it is engaged.
A thousand myths and legends tread Cornish soil,
As mermaids swim through the sea as it boils.
The ageless spirits of the land and the sea battle on,
As Cornish winter sings its mystic song.
Ancient waves buffet ancient shores.
So it has been and will be, forever and more.

Elizabeth O'Hara

CORNWALL

The country lanes so winding
the gorse upon the moor
the thatched roof on the cottage
wild flowers by the score.

The walk along the cliff tops
the seagulls' piercing cry
the blossom in the springtime
so pink against the sky.

The golden sand upon the shore
the brightness of the sun
the softness of the shadows
when day at last is done.

The place of many legends
that mystifies the mind
of castles and cathedral
that have stood the test of time.

No greater gift could I have
than the birthright that is mine
to be a son of Cornwall
now and for all time.

Elaine Tamblyn

CORNWALL (WHY DID NO-ONE HEAR?)

Why did no-one heed all the cries,
Of what used to be my countryside?
They sliced through me like a surgeon's knife,
For the tourists to come, without any strife.

Can you remember back years ago, when,
We didn't need tourists to help us to fend!
I was so very proud of my countryside then,
No scars to heal, and no bulldozing men.

I have high unemployment, and people who will pay,
To see *my* Lands End, (now taken away)
I now have the windmills perched high on my land,
And yet still I have sewerage, washed up on my sand!

My tin mines are gone now, dark waters run deep,
Those hard working miners, what jobs do they seek?
'We will retrain them,' our government cry,
To be what might I ask? (more pie in the sky)

I will never return to what used to be,
But *why* did you have to sacrifice me?
Where were those Cornishmen, 20,000 and true?
Where were you all, when I cried out for you?

J Middleton

THE RIGHT DECISION

A few years ago, my bridges burned
Away from home my face was turned.
Now, here in Cornwall I can see
A place where I really can be me.

No more, the rat race of London Town.
The daily grind that got me down.
Instead, the soul healing leisurely round
Of peace, and tranquillity I have found.

To take your ease on a sandy beach,
Beyond the hurly-burly's reach,
An idyllic setting? It had to be.
With sun, and sand, and sparkling sea

The kestrel flying in the clear blue sky
Above the rugged tors so high.
The springy turf beneath my feet
A view to where sky and moorland meet

I'm glad that I now live 'way down west'
Where the pace of life is best
I thank the Lord for that long ago day
When I came, I saw, and decided to stay.

John David Sams

A CORNISH SPRING

Oh how I view with pride
Upon my Cornish countryside.
When spring rushes in with indecent haste
Nature hates to arrive too late,
Transforming twigs to velvet bowers,
And bird song heard at all hours.
Soft buds of catkins can be seen
With golden trumpets heralding spring.
Soft winds caressing satin blossom
Transforming paths and edges soften
A foam of pink, flowing as a stream
And all around nature can be seen
Showing her best to all who dream.
Colours of bright and palest hues
Blowing away our winter blues.
Never a better sight can be seen
Than my Cornish countryside in spring.

Maureen Davis

STORM 89

P iercing cries of seagulls
O pen rolling sea
R ows of foaming breakers
T hrashing at the quay
H arbour walls of granite
L ined with slimy green
E xploding clouds of sea spray
V eil the violent scene
E ver moving waters
N ever ceasing scream

C rashing walls of water
O n cliffs and beach descend
R oaring their defiance
N ot sparing foe nor friend
W aves forever coming
A nd foaming sea crests fall
L ike hammers on an anvil
L oud, and flattening all.

Alan P Polley

HOLD A TOAST TO DEVON'S BOAST

Devon boasts
Magnificent coasts
Stretching far and wide around
Plymouth's gemstone
Without a doubt
Is the Hoe upon Plymouth Sound

Brixham is another place
A shining sapphire
Of nautical taste
Mooring ships such as the Golden Hind
A treasure unconcealed
For tourists to find

Bigbury, the place to be
Crystal waters
And a sandy shore
With cliffs that have stood
Since times of lore

Dawlish
A town simply to adore
With swingboat rides
Upon a beach
Of golden sands
Like sunset bleach

Clotted cream
Vanilla ice
Devon's recipe
Is so nice.

Stuart Higginson

PORT ISAAC HARBOUR

On the wall of the harbour
A small boy sits fishing
Whilst the gulls and the jackdaws
March a screaming parade.
They are waiting, impatient,
For anything dropped
They can swallow and take
To the next generation
Of seagulls and jackdaws
Back home on the cliff.
And what will you take
For your kith and kin
When you have to go home
To your life far from here?
Will it be a seashell
Plucked from the shore,
Or will it be memories
Of an old harbour wall
Where a small boy sits fishing
And feeding the gulls?

Amanda Aldridge

CORNWALL

Cornwall! My Cornwall! Means homeland to me,
Sands of pure gold reaching out for the sea.

Mountains of white, stand majestic and bold,
Strange legends and myths, fairytales to be told.

Rivers meander o'er gorseland and heath,
Some milky white, tinged with clay from beneath.

Relics of tin mines stand silent and still,
Ghosts of past miners the empty shafts fill.

From the harbour of Newlyn brave fishermen go
To harvest the sea from deep fathoms below.

Folk flock down to Cornwall for sun, sea and sand,
Tourism's the mainstay of our 'Duchy land'.

Pasties, fresh cream and stargazey pie,
Rich saffron cake, you really must try.

Couples retire here to find peace of mind,
They leave all the stress of the city behind.

Foreign countries to visit, places to roam,
When my travelling is over, to you, I'll come home.

Bernice Runnalls

MY CORNWALL

Cornwall is the place I call home
The place I return to, wherever I roam
Of pilchards and cream,
When away, things of which you dream.

The coastline, rugged and stark,
Outlined against skies, leaden and dark.
The sea mountainous, frothing and boiling,
Constantly searching, probing, never-ending, toiling.

Smashing against rocks for which time has stood still,
Looking to escape, with all its might and will.

Cornwall with its landscape fashioned by the elements,
With its trees gnarled, twisted and bent,
Untouched where man has only passed by,
And left its beauty unchanged, the vision of the eye.

Granite stones, some in circles, some on their own,
Mystic symbols from the past of festivals unknown.

Men who go to the sea in boats regardless of wind and rain
Their living to get, but not always for gain.

The miners in the bowels of the county,
Digging and delving for tin, or other bounty.

The farmer tilling and reaping, hoping for a big repast,
Following in the footsteps of generations past.

This is my Cornwall, of saffron buns, pasties and heavy cake,
Of food which only the Cornish can make.

Like the swallows who fly away with a swish,
I'll always return - simply because I'm Cornish.

R H Waters

DEVON

Devon is the place to dream
Of fluffy scones and loads of cream
Of pasties, hot from country stoves
Of Devon tuffs and cottage loaves
When you've eaten of this fayre
That of course is if you dare
Then you can sprint up all those hills
Or maybe take indigestion pills
Actually there is more to Devon
Many people's 'little heaven'
With coastal walks and golden sands
To trickle through those little hands
With hidden coves and wooded vales
And railway tracks with rusty rails
With sweeping moors, alone and bare
Where there's time to stop and stare

Irene Tapper

CREAM OF THE EARTH

The county of 'glorious' Devon,
is the perfect place to be,
for the folk are very friendly,
and there's idyllic scenery,
clotted cream and scrumpy,
is what the county's noted for,
so when you visit Devon,
take some, when you climb a tor,
Exeter's the capital
with its cathedral, standing tall,
but, visit Dartmoor when it's snowing,
and it's the bleakest sight of all,
there are many beauty spots,
some resorts are well loved too,
and tho' thatched cottages are old,
they're still as good as new,
many folk have travelled far,
across seas and oceans wide,
now old, they need tranquillity,
so they come to Devon to abide,
well known for a special accent,
oft' made fun of o'er the years,
you'll hear the aged Devonians
call everybody 'dears',
to folk who live in Devon, or,
if it's the county of your birth,
I'm sure you all will now agree,
It's the best county on this earth.

May Dabrowiecki

DEVON DELIGHTS

Plymouth Hoe is such a delight, the waterfront bustles
by day, and by night, craft large and small,
Frigates and schooners their mast's so tall.
Drakes Island is there too, where a great battle was
fought long ago,
Drake it is said, was busy, bowling on the Hoe.
The Spaniards are coming, he was told,
Just another battle, he said, to be put on hold.
The Mayflower steps just down the road, from where all
those poor souls sailed, so long ago.
The back-drop of the famous Dartmoor tors, stand tall,
back to the stone-age, so profound.
Can one keep one's foot, firmly on the ground.
A few miles away, is the English riviera.
The residents stand clear, from the annual invasion,
for the Grockels come, from every region,
from all parts, no matter what the season.
To look, and to wonder, at the scenery, beyond.
For all is so beautiful, calm, and serene.
A county with so much to offer, there is plenty to do,
Inclement weather, it doesn't matter.
A trip down the mine at Morwellham Quay.
Or a steam train ride from Buckfastleigh.
A river trip up the Dart;
Is only a taste, of what is in store,
For there is more, and more,
This is only the tip of an iceberg,
A region, so large, so profound,
It is a jewel in the crown, just waiting to be found.

Helen Phillips

TAKE A TRIP TO PLYMOUTH

Plymouth is a lovely place
with lots of things to do,
the lovely Barbican
and Plymouth Hoe
two places where every visitor should go,
visit the Theatre Royal
where there's always a good show
to see,
and then go to a café
for a lovely cream tea,
walk around the town
to buy a souvenir,
and maybe buy yourself
a new outfit to wear,
you could go on a boat trip
which leaves from the Mayflower steps
to see the naval ships,
a relaxing trip, you'll never forget
go to a restaurant for a lovely meal
to end your tiring day,
and then take home good memories
of when you came to stay.

Linda Casey

DEVON

I must go down to Devon again,
The urge is very strong,
Back to farmers and fisherfolk,
Back where I belong.

I must go down to Devon again,
Cider and cream to taste,
Might manage a trip to Honiton,
The home of such fine lace.

I must go down to Devon again,
To stroll on Plymouth Hoe,
To tread where Francis Drake trod,
Before defeating foe.

I must go down to Devon again,
And Brixham harbour see,
To chat to local boatmen,
Before they go to sea.

I must go down to Devon again,
To see the Cathedral grand,
The Guildhall too, in Exeter,
The Lammas' white-gloved hand.

I must go down to Devon again,
To join in Widdecombe Fair,
Across the moors wild ponies,
Gorse and heather there.

I've just been down to Devon again,
Fulfilled my childish dreams,
Wish I could have stayed longer,
But time to leave it seems . . .

Sue Goss

HOLBETON POINT

My favourite place on earth
Is walking distance from my home
Down and round a winding twisting lane
Pass the reeds and tall majestic purple rhododendrons
And behold! Shimmering in the morning sun
The river swirling left and right, wide and narrow
I sit and take in the tranquillity
Peace perfect peace
Then suddenly high above my head
The curlews scream and shout their eerie cry
Spring, summer, autumn, winter
Oh dear Lord, how I love it here.

Jean Jarrett

THE PRIDE OF DEVON

Devon is the place to be
If you're feeling low
Because it is so pretty there
Most everywhere you go.
There's all the little cottages
With roses round the door
And also lots of corner shops
That you can all explore.
There's churches with some steeples
That seem to reach the sky
And if you meet the locals too
You'll find they're rarely shy
But if you see the woods nearby
Then look inside them too
I'm sure you won't regret it
Because they're pretty too.
But if the country's not for you
Then all you have to do
Is drive a little further
As we've lots of towns here too.

Merilyn Gulley

DEVON

As I travel through Devon I see the hills and dales so green.
Far more than forty shades, they really must be seen.
There's also many shades of red and brown and gold.
The glory of Devon must be seen - for it cannot be told.
As I lay in my bed on a cold winter's night,
In my mind's eye I see once again Devon's glorious sight.

When I've travelled far, and I return to Devon,
I say silently within, 'For me this is truly heaven.'
There's no need to go abroad to see such a glorious sight.
Surely no other place on earth can give one such delight.
It's glory to see the ponies there on the moors.
To see the bluebells and count the tors.

The waters there at Burrator, of deepest blue;
The heather and gorse are of a perfect hue.
The carpet of bluebells there in the wood -
A sight for sore eyes, a sight that makes one feel good.
Strolling through Devon's winding paths among a mass array of trees,
One often comes across an 'olde worlde' cottage serving
Devon cream teas.

As one crosses the waters of the River Yealm
One realises it's one of the most glorious spots in England's realm.
The sun reflects golden into the Yealm's waters blue.
One cannot expect to find elsewhere, a more glorious view.
There are no jewels that one can compare
Against the colours of Devon's countryside so fair.

Strolling on through Devon, one finds many a shady nook.
There beside a stream or a babbling brook.
Devon's countryside is an artist's paradise.
The wonder of Devon is surely far beyond great price.
The hills in the distance - like a colourful patchwork quilt.
Only God could have created such glory, as it could not be built.

Christine Westgate

WEMBURY BAY

There's a little place in Devon
That means so much to me
It's right out in the country
And yet it's by the sea

There's a church upon the hillside
That's been viewed by many a ship
How many sailors have said a prayer
And been brought home safely from their trip.

A little island in the water sits
Not more than half a mile
And when the ships come upon it
I guess the sailors smile

For Plymouth Sound is not far away
Their loved ones soon they will see
They have waited and waited for this day
And what a grand day it will be.

I never go there anymore
The journey is too much for me
I miss the seat upon the shore
And the paddles in the sea.

I am almost as deaf as a post these days
But still I am able to see
The wonders of the countryside
And the storms upon the sea.

But still I have my memories
That will last me all my life
I can look back on the peaceful days
When this life seems full of strife

Lydia McCubbin

PRIDE OF DEVON

Pride of the Devon Lions are we;
Our spirits still roam far and free.
Frobisher, Hawkins, Raleigh and Drake -
Our mark on history did we make.

We sailed across the Spanish Main;
Renown and honour did we gain.
But back we came to Devon's shore -
Lionised - for evermore.

Annie Starkey

THE FARMER

Not sitting on the beach for pleasure,
Nor pursuing dreams of endless leisure.
You won't find him in outsize Reeboks,
Multi-coloured shorts or gaudy socks.

This fellow in overalls you'll find,
Going about his daily grind.
His handiwork abounds for all to see,
In patchwork fields you will agree.

When the sun is high, he seeks the shade,
Preferring to languish in a glade.
Not to say he doesn't work.
For from his tasks he does not shirk.

Travelling down any Devon lane
You'll see him gathering in the grain.
On his tractor to and fro,
With laden trailer often in tow.

On market days to town he goes,
Watching prices ebb and flow,
Of cattle, which he knows a thing or two,
Hoping to see a bargain through.

The salt of the earth indeed.
Respect of the countryside is his creed
For everything living,
To mother nature he is giving.

Douglas Dart

DARTMOOR

Where do tors like giant castles
  Stand against the sky,
And streams rush down the hillside
  Singing their lonely song?

Where do skylarks soar and sing
  All the summer through,
And summer wheatear dart along stone walls
  Feeding their young?

Where do ancient stone circles
  Hand in hand
Guard their dead
  And secrets of the past?

Where does purple heather bloom
  For just a little while,
Buzzing with bees
  And the sweet smell of honey?

Where do leats flow gently past
  Trout darting in their pure waters,
And sparkling, fragile dragonfly
  Rest awhile on their short journey?

Where do buzzards soar and cry
  The whole year through,
And the sun set, red, gold and purple
  When our journey's done?

Anne Hague

DARTMOOR

Land that goes on for miles on end
Never knowing what's behind the bend
Never knowing what tracks to take.
Listening to the sounds, the creatures make.
The sound of the rivers flowing wild
The sound of the wind so calm and mild.
Walkers climbing up Sheeps tor,
Not wondering where they're going no more.
When they finally reach the top
They sit upon a broken rock
Staring out at the beautiful view
Wondering if this life could be so true.

Carmen Weston

DEVON

Devon bore me, shaped, held me close;
This county that I love the most.
And every time I go away
I'm glad when I come home to stay.

My father was of Devon bred -
When I was small, the things he said
Of meadows, rivers, moors and seas
Made very special sense to me.

I breathe the essence of the seas,
And see the splendour of huge trees;
I wander on the gorse-grown heath
Or lie, a Devon bank beneath.

I thank the Lord for my homeland
And want the world to understand
That when I die my bones must rest
Beneath the soil I love the best.

Where rivers Exe and Dart will meet
My ghostly heart may give a beat;
And where the south west wind will be
It bears a speck of me to sea.

Elizabeth Mitchell

THE COMMUTERS

Exmouth . . .

waiting, tabloid men in tabloid suits
reading broadsheets to make a statement.
The driver will start his engine soon,
and the broadsheets will return

to the briefcase with sarnies and scant else.
The estuary is ripe this morning,
a green baize of weed, with boats
of all colours . . . yellow, green, brown, blue.

Lympstone Village . . .

expecting, the entire population should board here . . .
all six of them, leaving their haven
in the care of the tourists, who,
take great pleasure from two pubs and a post office.

Topsham . . .

resenting, wealthy people and beautiful people,
twenty pound notes for an eightypence fare people.
They don't care much for your type, they ignore,
and gaze expressionless towards . . .

Exeter . . .

belonging, home from home,
the destination but not the terminus.
The train will continue, north to Barnstaple or
south to Paignton, but I shall alight here with most others
and I shall return here presently.

Adrian Evans

THE DEVON COUNTRYSIDE

The countryside is the place to be,
Lots of beautiful things to see,
With grass so green and sky so blue.
Plants and flowers in every hue.

Rivers and streams a-flowing,
Hedges and trees a-growing,
Moorland walks are a pleasure,
With plenty of flora and fauna to treasure.

The birds and bees go flying by,
Dipping and diving in the sky,
With all these beautiful things to see,
Devon, certainly is the place to be.

Betty Colton

A DEVON FARM

Five o'clock in the morning,
The farmyard comes to life,
The farm cats wait patiently,
For milk from the farmer's wife.

Peace and quiet is shattered,
The crowing of the cock wakes everyone,
And along with his trusty sheep dog,
The farmer looks to see where his sheep have gone.

In the milk parlour, the herdsman,
Makes sure everything is sterile,
Buckets ready for milk for the calves,
His cows entering in single file.

The machinery is started up,
Udders cleaned before being connected,
Milk pumps through the pipes to the tank,
Being agitated till it is collected.

Tractors ploughing, getting the ground ready,
For oats, barley and wheat to be sown,
In August we will see the combine harvester,
Combining all that has grown.

The farmer's life is a hectic one,
He toils from dawn to dusk,
Tired and weary he gets ready for bed,
Removing from his hair, the last stray husk.

Glennis Horne

DEVONSHIRE DUMPLING

How lucky I am to be born in Devon,
The breathtaking views makes one think of heaven.
It's spring and the fields are vivid green,
Bluebells in the woods, a sight to be seen.

Tall hedges frame the winding lanes.
Sunlight sparkling on windowpanes.
Sheep and cows in fields so steep,
In the rushing river salmon leap.

Quaint thatched cottages in village streets,
Church and pubs where people meet.
Seagulls following plough, the earth so red
It's getting dimpsy time for bed.

Honeysuckle, scents the warm night air.
Foxes appearing from their lair.
Stars twinkling in a velvet sky,
Owls hooting in trees nearby.

Church clock striking the hour is late,
Call puss in, and shut the gate.
Gaze once more upon the tranquil scene
And realise how privileged I have been.

Peggy Moore

QUILT ME A COUNTY

Quilt me a county, patchwork of green,
Threaded with rivers and hedges between.
Stitch the red furrows, use brown for the moors,
Embroider the flowers, appliqué the tors.

Place proud in the centre
Of this work of art
The splendid cathedral
At Exeter's heart.

Take blue for the borders and lace for the foam,
To quilt me a picture of my Devon home.
Then wherever I travel I'll sing Devon's praise,
And wrap my quilt round me to dream Devon days.

Marian Lancaster

LOOKING WESTWARDS

From my window looking westwards, a vast expanse of trees and moor,
Distant hills a purple hump, rising from the autumn floor
Above the mist that wreaths the trees with naked bark in winter's cold,
Gnarled oak, beech like sentries, the outline stark and bold.
From my window looking westwards, a scenic view of countryside
Where creatures of various species, emerge to feed, and hide.
Bushes of a different hue, clothed with leaves and golden,
A forest, huge, of dark green pine against the far horizon.
From my window looking westwards, cattle, local farmers' stock,
Streams like ribbon threading through the ancient clefts of rock.
Brown and dead a patch of fern, heath covered by fallen leaves
Moulding in the autumn chill, whipped by winds that blow and tease.
From my window looking westwards I see roads as bits of string
Winding through the hills and dales, toy-like traffic, creeping.
There's a village, church and steeple tucked away in woody hollow,
Farms in lonely state with just a narrow lane to follow.
From my window looking westwards, once again a changing scene
Always restless Mother Nature, rain and wind now fresh and keen.
When I awake and draw the curtains never tiring of this sight
If only you could see it also, this Devonshire, so green, so right.

Patricia Evans

MY DEVON

Devon to me, means so many things,
Sheltered valleys, thatched cottages, and sunlit streams,
The wild rolling moors that go on forever,
The animals and plants that live amongst the heather,
To stand on the highest tor, and look out over land and sea
All around is natural beauty, it's a place I love to be.

To walk through the sleepy countryside,
And stop by in the village inn,
To be welcomed by the locals,
With good food, beer and a grin.

The fishing boats that gently bob,
Down by the harbour side,
The cries of the hungry seagull,
The coming in of the evening tide.

Devon, has a lovely city too!
And Plymouth is its name,
Where Drake played bowls upon the Hoe,
But the Spanish interrupted his game!

So, altogether for me,
Devon is such a special place,
The history and the beauty,
Is here for all the human race.

Yvette Mullis

THE WHOLE DEVON SCENE

Devon is one of the places
When you've been once
You will come back again
For you see it has so much to offer
Although we do have too much rain
We have history to share if you want to
There's the Barbican, Drake and much more
We have sea and the Hoe and Drake's island
Or coach trips to visit the moors
We have pubs, olde worlde, the theatre
Restaurants, cafes the like
We have quite a few places to visit
To please and a varied night-life
Best of all there is always a welcome
Try the cream teas in Devon, they're great
The ice-cream is something of wonder
And the pasties would fill any plate
There is beautiful countryside waiting
A city that's so fresh and clean
So do come and visit us sometime
Be part of the whole Devon scene

Jeanette Gaffney

CRANMERE POOL

Atop the moors, beyond the trackways,
sit mired pools within the plain;
staring wind cuts through the landscape
midst tussock grass beswept with rain.
Heather covered granite huddles
ensconced in ferns, green forts of main,
about the hawthorns black and blossom
gambols mist in cotton frame.
O'er all stands the dewed rock slickly,
on the skyline shadows gain;
sun drops down to salmon ending
yet all of stone and life remain.
In this place the seasons tarry
where all's so diff'rent,
yet the same.

Steve Newbury

THREE MILES OF TAMAR

Sparkling pebbles, dancing light and laughter,
Bubbling with gaiety, life and living, after
Passing through the rapids on your course.
Trout lurk within deep pools and an old horse
Plods across his pasture to drink sweet water.
And you run on gurgling, to back and quarter
Your way through verdant hills and valleys,
Pressing on in little runs and rallies,
Merrily leaping miniature waterfalls,
You grow and burgeon, passing inns and village halls
Until, broad and placid, you pursue your way
Through sleepy country on a drowsy summer's day.

Nick Spargo

SILENT WATCHER

I stand erect on a barren hill,
But for the breeze all is still.
The dying sun casts rays of blood
On the land laid out before me.
It descends beyond the distant horizon,
And enveloping night closes in.

James Spargo

DEVON DELIGHTS

When you are in Devon,
Travel to Haldon Moor.
A little piece of country,
Like you've not seen before.
In late summer, lovely purple heather
Fritillary butterflies by the score.

Out over, upon Exmoor,
The heather is there too,
You will feel idyllic
Under skies of blue.
Then, in the lovely Doone valley,
You will want to stay and tarry.

Little streams, thatched cottages,
Beaches, long and golden,
Up, near to the Braunton Burrows,
Where the sea waves fill the hollows:
Trees dip into the bouldered Lyn river:
Look; red deer will set your heart a-quiver.

The river Exe, it begins here,
Tumbling down to lower reaches,
Until it reaches Exeter and on
To Dawlish Warren, Exmouth beaches.
The lovely Teign and Dart and Tamar
Along their banks, a wildlife treasure.

Fields of green and yellow grasses,
High, red cliffs at Shaldon.
Wednesdays, summertime on the green
A play staged by the lads and lasses:
Here, Punch and Judy still exists,
Childhood scenes we can't resist.

Pearl Mansell (Exeter)

BATH IN BLOOM

How beautiful the city looks
Adorned in its array
Flowers displayed everywhere
Makes streets and gardens and parks so gay.

One is bound to appreciate and admire
The lovely scene all around.
Hats off to you men who
Worked so hard to make
Bath the city of bloom.

Edna Pine

A FIELD IN SOMERSET

I wish for you the tender tread across the field of morning;

The silver trail abandoned,
The even flow of loss dismissed 'neath
Hide of boughs irriguous.
Branches, spent, behold the seeds,
The quickening eye within,
I wish for you the place of morning,
I wish for us the morrow.

J C Aston

SOMERSET SPRING

Down to Wells
Our favourite way
Spring and sun beckons us
Showers, cloud, May time
Pink and white, the hedgerow dressed
Golden daffodils in cottage gardens
Distant tor on faraway hill
Celtic mystery all around
Chewton Mendip, Green Ore and Priddy
The Fosseway shines
The rainbow touches earth
May in Somerset
The *only place* to be

Vera Dyer

SOMERSET

The swirling mists round Glastonbury Tor
In ghostly swathes eradicate the base
The square-shaped edifice atop stands proud
A beacon to the pilgrims to this place

And farther down the road the Festival
At Pilton makes its urgent presence felt
From every walk of life they congregate
As into one huge throng the people melt.

A different kind of tower from Glastonb'ry
Is starkly outlined on the Channel coast
The nuclear plant entrenched at Hinkley Point
Made Somerset, reluctantly, its host.

The River Parrett boasts its little Bore
At Bridgwater a source of huge delight
To children on the bridge who watch the scene
And revel in this unfamiliar sight.

A county rich in pastoral pursuits
Of basket-making, thatching, digging peat,
Where Alfred, King of Wessex, stayed awhile
At Athelney, a haven and retreat.

This gentle county also had to bear
The stains of battle on its quiet land
To Sedgemoor came the Duke of Monmouth's troops
To find themselves defeated and out-manned.

So rich in folklore and in history
A fascinating tapestry of time
To delve into the past is wonderful
To live here in the present is sublime.

J Wenmoth

OUR TOWN, WESTON-SUPER-MARE

Our town is very special because it's by the sea,
With bracing winds and distant waves that never come too near,
Many folk come to the town and have a good look round,
With shops and clubs and cafés in every street they're found,
We wonder what's the attraction but now it's plain to see
It's fresh air and friendliness and 'a nice cup of tea',
So why we grumble every day to try and pass the crowds,
Remember we're the lucky ones we have this town all year round,
So with the summer coming spare a thought for city folk,
They come here 'cause it's healthy and at least that can't be bought!

Dympna Slattery

WINTER IN THE ABBEY

Footsteps crunch on the frost trimmed grass
fresh prints on virgin ground.
No saint has trod this way today;
Yet, in centuries past
once trod the saints who first discovered
this hallowed place.
What were they seeking?
What did they find in this Isle of Avalon?

Stately trees stretch their bare branches up
into the cool pale blue of a still winter sky.
Where is life?
Nestled, warm beneath their cushioning bark,
sheltered from the icy blasts.
So we too come close to God,
in retreat from the storms of life,
like ships heading for peaceful harbours.

Come all for respite from life's trials;
Time for refreshment; Renewed,
full of vigour to face once again
all that the winter of our lives can fling
into faces stinging with battling the cold;
Stepping boldly forward
as once did the Holy men
who trod this winter place.

Val Flint-Johnson

ZUMERZET ... OOOARRRR!

Come and visit 'Zumerzet', it's a place you'd want to see.
Being rural and quiet, it's where you'd want to be.
Get away from hassles, that cause daily stress and strife
Visit deeper 'Zumerzet', for your stress and hassle-free life.
Please don't think of 'Zumerzet' just as 'pig farms and sheep'.
Once you've visited this area, the peace you'll want to keep.

Louise Brown

PRIDE OF SOMERSET

There's such a lot in Somerset as many will agree,
The rolling hills and country lanes and much to do and see.
There's something here for everyone from caves to buildings grand,
While much is steeped in history and legend lends a hand.

It's noted for its cheeses and strawberries luscious too,
While cider, strong and potent is a popular local 'brew'.
But the heart of this lovely county are the beautiful Mendip Hills,
Whose calm and gentle slopes uplift and with peace the heart doth fill.

We should be proud of Somerset and not its beauty spoil,
As many seek a refuge from rush and work and toil.
For life's concrete jungle brings stress of many kinds,
And the healing balm of nature may soon be hard to find.

F L Brain

UNTITLED

To live in Devon we are truly blessed
It really contains all that's best
Thatched cottages, villages, Devon cream teas,
Picture postcard images, many of these
Fishing boats, nests drying in the sun,
Holiday photos for everyone,
Seagulls sweeping calling each other
Plenty of food here come down brother.
Water sports and moorland walks
Ways to spend our leisure
Do we ever stop and realise
We're surrounded with such treasure
Breathtaking scenery promotes
A peaceful mood
Sweet breeze blowing
Insects humming, an idyllic interlude
With its climate so mild
Even the weather smiles
On this beautiful part of the British Isles.

Joan E Bartlett

DEVON'S JEWEL

Dartmoor has a magic
a wonderful mystique,
Her magnetism draws you
with a power that's unique;
From distant hills she beckons
with beauty and beguile,
To challenge and seduce
in her inimitable style.

Bearing no discrimination
for culture, race or creed,
She will take us in her arms,
satisfy our every need;
Inviting us to wander
lay our troubles at her feet,
Then engages our affections;
the consummation is complete.

A love affair with Dartmoor
is unlike any other,
Such is the vibrant power
of this wondrous earth mother;
She is strong, yet she is fragile
and never must succumb,
To the foibles of man:
she must always over-come.

Margaret Vincent

INFORMATION

We hope you have enjoyed reading this book - and that you will continue to enjoy it in the coming years.

If you like reading and writing poetry drop us a line, or give us a call, and we'll send you a free information pack.

Write to :-
Anchor Books Information
1-2 Wainman Road
Woodston
Peterborough
PE2 7BU
(01733) 230761